131

The Sad Squirrel

By JENNA LAFFIN

Illustrated by BRIAN HARTLEY

Music Arranged and Produced by MARK OBLINGER

CANTATA
LEARNING

WWW.CANTATALEARNING.COM

CANTATA
LEARNING

Published by Cantata Learning
1710 Roe Crest Drive
North Mankato, MN 56003
www.cantatalearning.com

A note to educators and librarians from the publisher: Cantata Learning has provided the following data to assist in book processing and suggested use of Cantata Learning product.

Publisher's Cataloging-in-Publication Data
Prepared by Librarian Consultant: Ann-Marie Begnaud
Library of Congress Control Number: 2015958172
    The Sad Squirrel
    Series. Me, My Friends, My Community : Songs about Emotions
    By Jenna Laffin
    Illustrated by Brian Hartley
    Summary: Learn about feeling sad in the song.
    ISBN: 978-1-63290-550-5 (library binding/CD)
    ISBN: 978-1-63290-644-1 (paperback/CD)
Suggested Dewey and Subject Headings:
    Dewey: E 152.4
    LCSH Subject Headings: Seasons – Juvenile literature. | Emotions – Juvenile literature. | Seasons – Songs and music – Texts. |
Emotions – Songs and music – Texts. | Seasons – Juvenile sound recordings. | Emotions – Juvenile sound recordings.
    Sears Subject Headings: Emotions. | Seasons. | School songbooks. | Children's songs. | World music.
    BISAC Subject Headings: JUVENILE NONFICTION / Social Topics / Emotions & Feelings. | JUVENILE NONFICTION
/ Music / Songbooks. | JUVENILE NONFICTION / Concepts / Seasons.

Book design and art direction, Tim Palin Creative
Editorial direction, Flat Sole Studio
Music direction, Elizabeth Draper
Music arranged and produced by Mark Oblinger

Printed in the United States of America in North Mankato, Minnesota.
072016   0335CGF16

ACCESS THE MUSIC!

SCAN CODE WITH MOBILE APP

CANTATALEARNING.COM

Sometimes we get sad when things change. It's okay to feel that way. It's okay to be sad when something you like goes away. Just remember, there is always something new around the corner.

Turn the page to see how Crow cheers up Squirrel. Remember to sing along!

Sad little Squirrel
sat in a tree,
crying and **sighing**,
unhappy as could be.

Then Crow flew by and asked,
"Squirrel, why do you **frown**?"

8

"Because summer is gone, and leaves are falling down."

"The flowers have all gone.
The bears have gone to sleep.

The wind is cold and lonely."
Then Squirrel began to **weep**.

"Sad little Squirrel," said Crow,
"don't be blue.

The seasons change.
It's time for something new."

11

"Don't you love the snow, Squirrel?
And **moonlight** on the ice?

And snowflakes and presents?
Wintertime is quite nice."

"The flowers are now sleeping,
but when the winter's through,
springtime comes creeping back.
It's time for something new!"

"Sad little Squirrel," said Crow,
"don't be blue.

The seasons change.
It's time for something new."

Then Squirrel began to smile
and dance in the sun.

"I was sad for a while,
but now I'm glad. Look what's to come!"

"The seasons change.
I won't feel blue.

I'll tell my friends when I feel sad
and wait for something new."

So remember happy Squirrel,
and don't feel blue.

The seasons change, and feelings change.
It's time for something new!

SONG LYRICS
The Sad Squirrel

Sad little Squirrel
sat in a tree,
crying and sighing,
unhappy as could be.

Then Crow flew by and asked,
"Squirrel, why do you frown?"

"Because summer is gone,
and leaves are falling down."

"The flowers have all gone.
The bears have gone to sleep.

The wind is cold and lonely."
Then Squirrel began to weep.

"Sad little Squirrel," said Crow,
"don't be blue.

The seasons change.
It's time for something new."

"Don't you love the snow, Squirrel?
And moonlight on the ice?

And snowflakes and presents?
Wintertime is quite nice."

"The flowers are now sleeping,
but when the winter's through,
springtime comes creeping back.
It's time for something new!"

"Sad little Squirrel," said Crow,
"don't be blue.

The seasons change.
It's time for something new."

Then Squirrel began to smile
and dance in the sun.

"I was sad for a while,
but now I'm glad. Look what's to come!"

"The seasons change.
I won't feel blue.

I'll tell my friends when I feel sad
and wait for something new."

So remember happy Squirrel,
and don't feel blue.

The seasons change, and feelings change.
It's time for something new!

The Sad Squirrel

World
Mark Oblinger

Verse 2
Then Crow flew by and asked,
"Squirrel, why do you frown?"
"Because summer is gone,
and leaves are falling down."

Verse 3
"The flowers have all gone.
The bears have gone to sleep.
The wind is cold and lonely."
Then Squirrel began to weep.

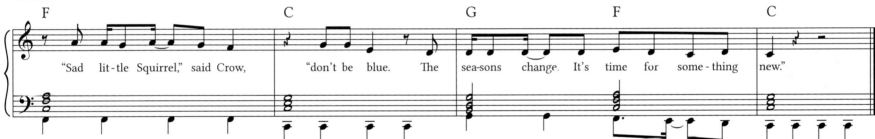

Verse 4
"Don't you love the snow, Squirrel?
And moonlight on the ice?
And snowflakes and presents?
Wintertime is quite nice."

Verse 5
"The flowers are now sleeping,
but when the winter's through,
springtime comes creeping back.
It's time for something new!"

Chorus

Verse 6
Then Squirrel began to smile
and dance in the sun.
"I was sad for a while,
but now I'm glad. Look what's to come!"

Verse 7
"The seasons change.
I won't feel blue.
I'll tell my friends when I feel sad
and wait for something new."

Chorus
So remember happy Squirrel,
and don't feel blue.
The seasons change, and feelings change.
It's time for something new!

GLOSSARY

frown—to make a sad or unhappy face

moonlight—light from the moon

sighing—taking deep breaths and letting them out

springtime—the season of spring

weep—to cry

wintertime—the season of winter

GUIDED READING ACTIVITIES

1. Think of a time you felt sad. What made you feel that way? What did you do when you felt sad?

2. At the beginning of this song, Squirrel is frowning. On a sheet of paper, draw a face with a frown. When you are done, flip the paper over. Now draw the same face with a smile!

3. On a piece of paper, write down things that make you happy. They can be favorite foods or fun things you like to do.

TO LEARN MORE

Aboff, Marcie. *Everyone Feels Sad Sometimes*. Minneapolis, MN: Picture Window Books, 2010.

Law, Felicia. *Feelings*. Chicago: Norwood House Press, 2016.

Nichols, Cheyenne. *Sad Is…* Mankato, MN: Capstone Press, 2012.

Thomas, Isabel. *Dealing with Feeling Sad*. Mankato, MN: Heinemann-Raintree, 2013.